101 SAFE

Internet

SITES FOR KIDS

CHRISTOPHER D. HUDSON

BARBOUR
PUBLISHING, INC.
Uhrichsville, Ohio

101 SAFE

Internet

SITES FOR KIDS

Developed and produced by the Livingstone Corporation.

Cover design by Robyn Martins.

Published by Barbour Publishing, Inc., P.O. Box 719, Uhrichsville, Ohio 44683

Check out Barbour's exciting web site at: http://www.barbour-books.com

Member of the
Evangelical Christian
Publishers Association

Printed in the United States of America.

DEDICATION

To Caleb and Ryan:
I pray that books like this one will help you
be in the world, but not of it.

CONTENTS

INTRODUCTION

Welcome to *101 Safe Internet Sites for Kids,* an important tool for parents who want to help their children safely navigate the best of the web. This book will help you and your kids feel more comfortable with the Internet, help you find the sites that are interesting and helpful to them, and help you control their on-line experience.

This book *can't,* however, take the place of a careful parent. The Internet changes rapidly (web sites come and go, and on-line communities are bought and sold), so we've done our best to review these sites and to ensure that they are suitable for all ages. We've alerted you if a site might need special warnings.

We can't guarantee that our "safe" standards match yours, however. It's possible that content or advertising approved by webmasters may cause us to remove a site from our recommended list. We'll be keeping up with the sites listed, but your comments on them are welcome, too. You may e-mail your comments or site suggestions to *hudson@techie.com*

Remember, *no book or filter can replace an informed, conscientious parent.* God bless your efforts to be a wired, effective Christian in the twenty-first century. Happy surfing!

CHRISTOPHER D. HUDSON

FREQUENTLY ASKED QUESTIONS

FAQ (Frequently Asked Questions)

Experienced surfers and newcomers to the net have important questions. So, before you begin surfing, check out these answers to the most frequently asked questions:

Is the Internet safe?

If used wisely, yes. But you should take a number of steps to protect yourself on-line:

Never allow your children to give personal information (last name, age, passwords, name of their school, and their physical location) to strangers. Consider making up a "handle" or a fun pretend name they can use while on-line.

Establish clear rules about: 1) the kinds of sites your kids can and can't visit; 2) on-line chats; and 3) on-line discussion boards.

Practice safe surfing habits by using a web-filtering program, and follow the other points listed on the next page.

Isn't the Internet filled with pornography, violence, and gambling?

While such sites exist, they actually make up a small percentage of the Internet. We reviewed thousands of sites while preparing this book. By practicing the safe-surfing suggestions we've outlined on the next page, we never once opened or stumbled across any pornographic sites. Sure, those sites exist, but you can steer clear of them.

Should I allow my children access to the Internet?

We think so. Children quickly adjust to the Internet and learn to "surf " more easily than adults. We believe that part of being an effective Christian in the twenty-first century will mean understanding and being able to navigate our world—including the Internet.

Does the good outweigh the bad?

Yes. While a child's Internet use requires parental guidance and clear guidelines, the Internet can help your child grow, learn more, and have some good, clean fun.

TIPS FOR SAFE SURFING

You should stay clear of some Internet sites. These sites can be avoided by taking a few simple steps. These tips will help you enjoy the Internet.

Use filtering software. This is your first line of defense. We suggest http://www.netnanny.com or http://www.browsesafe.com.

Talk to your children about the kinds of sites that are "off-limits."

Surf with your kids. Be near the computer when they are on-line so that you can monitor where they go.

Keep your computer centrally located, in a well-trafficked room in your house. Isolated or secluded locations are not easy for a parent to monitor.

Limit the number of hours each day that your child is on-line. Remember, the Internet can be addictive. Even innocent surfing can become a big time waster.

Keep your children's last name private. Be sure they understand the importance of *not* posting their last name on a message board or revealing it in chat rooms.

Have an E-mail address they can use when they register at different sites (this should be different than the E-mail address they give to friends). Some sites sell E-mail addresses to third parties who generate "junk" E-mail. Much of the junk E-mail is not appropriate for children. You probably won't want junk E-mail going to your child's inbox.

Make sure the guidelines are clear. Some parents let their kids draw up and sign a contract explaining rules and consequences.

Never download programs or E-mail from the Internet without a good anti-virus system installed. We recommend Norton Antivirus, which can be downloaded from http://www.symantec.com.

CHRISTIAN
SITES

KidsBible.Com

http://www.kidsbible.com

It's a Bible! It's a web site! KidsBible.com is actually both. Cartoon characters Skweek and Tagg  take you through this new, exciting site. These characters lead you through Bible stories and offer games to play. This site also lets you write and post lessons you've learned from the Bible and encourage kids all over the world.

Notes

_____

_____

_____

_____

CRAFTS FOR KIDS

http://www.makingfriends.com

At Making Friends you'll find lots of creative activities for kids of all ages. You can quickly find Bible crafts, scout pages, bead patterns, and holiday fun.

PRAYER AND HOMEWORK

http://www.kids-teens.org

This site is a perfect blend between just plain old fun and Christian-centered content. At this site you will find on-line testimonies, kids' home pages, and devotionals for kids, as well as games, fun pages, and more. You can do many things here from getting homework help to joining a prayer chain.

GOD AND HIS CREATION

www.christiananswers.net/kids/home.html

Learn about God while you explore his creation. This site shows you what you can learn about God while studying  animals or learning about other cultures. You'll also have fun playing a number of games and activities. Listen to sounds from the rain forest and watch video clips of some cool animals.

NOTES

_____

_____

_____

_____

_____

Kidspot

http://www.kidspot.org

Did you know that
God can use you no
matter how old you
are? Here's a site
that was partially
constructed by kids
to encourage other kids. You'll find videos to
watch, stories to read, Bible trivia, jokes, and
riddles. You'll read about the greatest story
ever told as well as be given the opportunity to
join a Mailbox Club where you get free Bible
lessons by mail.

Notes

_____

_____

_____

_____

VEGGIE TALES

http://www.bigidea.com

From the makers of Veggie Tales, this site is packed with fun games, stories, and activities. Check out video clips, fight crime with Larry Boy, or learn more about upcoming Veggie Tales events.

NOTES

_____

_____

_____

_____

_____

_____

Christian Kids' Links

http://home.netministries.org/kids.htmls

This site links you with Christian and other wholesome sites. Sites included are appropriate for kids and are devotional, educational, or just plain fun.

Underwater Fun

http://www.angelfire.com/on/nadya

This unusual underwater treasure hunt is just plain fun. Search the underwater world for the greatest treasure you can ever find.

KIDS' BIBLE NEWS

http://www.kidsnewspress.com

Here are Bible stories written as if they were newspaper stories. These stories bring Bible accounts to life. After reading the stories, do the suggested activities to help drive the story home.

NOTES

_____

_____

_____

_____

_____

_____

_____

GOD'S WORLD FOR KIDS

http://www.gwnews.com

A children's version of *World* magazine offers coverage and analysis of world news from a Christian point of view.

KIDS WEB

http://www.etcc.org/kidsweb2.htm

This site has lots of java style games that you don't find in many other places. Play against the computer in "Rock, Paper, Scissors," UFO Attack, Connect 4, Smash the Smiley, Wermz, and Pac-Man. It's lots of fun, and it's all a service of the Greater Tulsa Christian Church.

CHRISTIAN KIDS' FUN CENTER

http://www.calvary.com/beantown

This Christian site allows you to solve mysteries with your hosts Willie, Grace, Furball, and Flop. While on the site you'll interact with Bible stories and puzzles and then find cool stuff to make.

NOTES

_____

_____

_____

_____

_____

_____

_____

321 PENGUINS

http://www.321penguins.com

Those wacky pen-
guins are on-line,
too! Spend some
time with Zidgel,
Midgel, Fidgel, and
Kevin. This new
series from Big Ideas is full of faith, fun and
flightless birds.

GOSPELCOM

http://www.gospelcom.net/gci/kc

Here is a corner of GospelCom, the famous
Christian site, that is dedicated to kids, fun,
and games.

McGee and Me!

http://www.mcgeeandme.com

Once on-line you'll find the *McGee and Me* coloring book, screen savers, games, and more. You can also read more about the series.

Notes

_____

_____

_____

_____

_____

_____

CLUBHOUSE

http://www.clubhousemagazine.org

This magazine and web site (created by Focus on the Family) is jammed with Bible lessons,  fiction, and real-life stories from today. You'll also find puzzles, jokes, crafts, recipes, and almost anything else that interests a Christian kid.

CHRIST-CENTERED MALL

http://www.christcenteredmall.com/kids

The owners of this site aggressively work to keep bad influences away. One great feature is its family-friendly chat room.

ADVENTURES IN ODYSSEY

http://www.whitsend.org

At the official site
of this cartoon
series, you'll find
the latest news
from Odyssey, test
your skills and cre-

ativity, go behind the scenes, and listen to
sound effects.

NOTES

_____

_____

_____

_____

_____

_____

Watch Christian TV

http://www.lifeaudio.com/lightsource/
partners/jesusfilm/

Ever watch a whole movie while on-line? This site offers you the chance to watch an hour-long movie, *The Story of Jesus for Children*

Christianity On-line—Kids

http://www.christianitytoday.com/kids

This Christian site also offers on-line Bible stories, Bible studies, and quizzes. Be sure to check out the on-line games. (Water Balloon Drop is a favorite of many!) This site also links you to other great games all over the Internet. You'll also find areas to help you get through your homework.

GUIDEPOSTS FOR KIDS

http://www.gp4k.com/index.shtm

This site is the home
to the well-known
magazine *Guideposts
for Kids*. This site
offers good advice,
inspirational stories,
fun games, and coloring pages. You'll also find a
post office to send E-cards to family and
friends.

NOTES

_____

_____

_____

_____

_____

God's Truth in Comics

http://www.kidzweb.org

Do you laugh enough while you learn about God? Here are some great cartoons that will teach you more about Him.

Children's Sonshine Network

http://www.gospelcom.net/csn

The Children's Sonshine Network links together radio programs that you can enjoy while on-line. Now you can have some great entertainment no matter what's on the radio where you live!

BIBLE STORIES WITH A TWIST

http://www.essex1.com/people/paul/Bible.html

Read paraphrased Bible stories that help you better understand God's Word. The story-teller is a cartoonist,  so you'll find a lot of good, funny cartoons sprinkled throughout the site.

NOTES

_____

_____

_____

_____

_____

Little Dogs on the Prairie

http://www.fancymonkey.com

Here's the popular kids' series that teaches faith and values. Since this is the same group that produced the Jungle Jam Radio Show, you can go on-line and get more familiar with the series or take a quiz to see how big a fan you really are.

Donut Man

http://www.donutmanmusic.com

Listen to the Donut Man songs, e-mail Duncan, or find out why "life without Jesus is like a donut."

NOTES

_____

_____

_____

_____

_____

_____

_____

_____

_____

_____

_____

_____

_____

_____

LEARNING SITES

ART FOR KIDS

http://artforkids.miningco.com/kids/
artforkids/mbody.htm

Here's a terrific starting place for kids who love art. Whether it's making a card or more advanced arts and crafts, this is a good starting point.

NOTES

_____

_____

_____

_____

_____

_____

_____

BILL NYE THE SCIENCE GUY

http://www.billnye.com

Science is fun for almost everyone when Bill Nye is the teacher. Surf this site to learn amazing things and download over forty interesting experiments that are safe to do at home.

RAIN FOREST

http://www.ran.org/ran/kids_action/

Learn about the people, plants, and animals that live in rainforests. This interactive site lets you ask questions, find answers, and uncover ways that kids can help protect the rain forest.

FUNSCHOOL

http://www.funschool.com

Learning is fun when you're at Funschool.
This site caters to
children from pre-
school through
sixth grade.
Funschool.com's
entertaining, educa-

tional content helps younger ages learn to
read, match, and count. Older surfers can discover more about history and outer space.

NOTES

_____

_____

_____

_____

_____

CHILDREN'S PLAYROOM

http://www.entourages.com/barbs/
    playroom.htm

This site is a good starting point as it links you to many books you can read on-line. Start here to read some *Peter Rabbit, Theodore Tug Boat, Winnie the Pooh,* and *Planet Zoom.* Also features link to school and non-school web sites, children's ministries, and general kid-fun sites.

THE LEARNING KINGDOM

http://www.learningkingdom.com

This site works hard trying to be the best learning center on the web. Some unique features at this site include the Word of the Day, Cool Fact of the Day, and Today in History. The Learning Kingdom hosts an on-line academy to encourage little minds and an on-line playground to offer the breaks everyone needs.

AMERICA'S STORY

http://www.americaslibrary.gov/cgi-bin/page.cgi

Talk about a library. . . . This is the kids' section of the official Library of Congress web site—full of fun and interesting information on Amazing Americans, the states, popular activities, and more. History doesn't have to be dull—you'll agree as you navigate this site.

NOTES

_____

_____

_____

_____

_____

_____

_____

INTERNATIONAL KIDS

http://www.kids-space.org

This site is geared
for younger kids
and uses the latest
in education to
encourage young-
sters to use their

imaginations. You'll also learn more about
children from around the world and read their
interesting stories.

DON'T JUST SURF

http://www.looklearnanddo.com

At the Look, Learn, and Do web site, kids can
read great books, learn interesting facts, and
build fun projects with easy-to-follow, illustrated
plans.

After School Clubhouse

http://www.eduplace.com/kids

This Houghton Mifflin site offers free games, activities, and resources for kids studying math, reading, social studies, and science. The site also offers some material from the company's textbooks to help make this site useful for young scholars.

Notes

_____

_____

_____

_____

_____

_____

_____

THE YUCKIEST SITE ON THE INTERNET

http://www.yucky.com

This is one of the most popular science sites on the Internet. Kids can choose from Yucky Fun and Games, Ask Wendell, Gross and Cool Body, Worm World, or Roach World. Kids learn about the life of a roach, explore smells and sounds made by the human body, and discover the fun-filled activities that bring science to life.

LEARNINGPLANET

http://www.learningplanet.com

This site is so much fun you'll be surprised how much you're learning. This site features fun, interactive, learning activities and games for kids. Activities are divided into Pre-kindergarten, grades 1–3, and grades 4–6. Planet Mom is a section of the site that allows parents to find the best activities for their kids.

NOTES

_____

_____

_____

_____

_____

_____

ASTRONOMY FOR KIDS

http://www.frontiernet.net/~
kidpower/astronomy.html

What's a comet?
Why doesn't the sun
burn up? What's the
moon made out of?
The answers to these
and other questions

can be found at this simple, easy-to-navigate site.

DOLE 5 A DAY

http://www.dole5aday.com

Enjoy learning about fruit. Hosts like Amber
Orange and Barney Broccoli make food more
fun than you thought possible.

YUM OR YUCK?

http://www.kidsfood.org

Is it true to say, "You are what you eat?" Maybe. Log on to check out how good your eating habits are. You'll never look at your dinner plate the same way.

NOTES

_____

_____

_____

_____

_____

THE WHITE HOUSE

http://www.whitehouse.gov/kids

Kids are often interested in the president. This official White House site has a special section for kids, which gives a history of the house and tells about the children and pets who have lived there.

THE "WHY FILES?"

http://whyfiles.org

Why does the world have earthquakes? Why do people get sick? Why does it snow? Why do the seasons change? If you you're inquisitive, you may *need* this site. This site gives the scientific background of the natural events that you hear and read about in the news.

THE NINE PLANETS

http://seds.//pl.arizona.edu/
nineplanets/nineplanets/
nineplanets.html

Take a multimedia tour of our solar system. This resource gives an overview of each planet and moon in our solar system. Each page has text and pictures; some have sounds and movies. This site will blast you out of this world.

NOTES

_____

_____

_____

_____

_____

_____

PBS KIDS

http://pbskids.com

Lots of kids love
the programs on
PBS: *Barney,*
Mister Rogers,
Dragon Tales,
Teletubbies, and so

on. If you love kid shows, this site will easily
keep your interest.

FUNBRAIN

http://www.funbrain.com

Funbrain is known for making learning fun.
Travel to Funbrain to play Math Baseball,
Grammar Gorillas, and Math Car Racing. All
age groups will find custom learning activities.

Discovery!

http://kids.discovery.com

What do you think it is like to live on a space station? How do children in other parts of the world live? What do bugs eat? The best info from the Discovery Channel has been translated into an informative site for kids.

Notes

_____

_____

_____

_____

_____

KIDS' ZONE

http://www.pfizerfunzone.com

This fun site, created by Pfizer (a big drug company), is for children ages eight to thirteen. It's a place to learn  about the science of medicine, play games, and do experiments at home. This site will let you travel back in time to experience the history of science, learn about discoveries that have changed our lives, and explore things you cannot see (like microbes!)

SPORTS ILLUSTRATED FOR KIDS

http://www.sikids.com

At sikids.com you can play cool sports games, vote for your favorite teams and players, and send sports E-cards! While you're at the site, watch *SI*'s own kids' cartoon shows and use the birthday finder to find out who shares your special day.

NOTES

_____

_____

_____

_____

_____

_____

TIME FOR KIDS

http://www.timeforkids.com

This site presents *Time* magazine quality news in a way that kids can understand. This interactive site  brings current events to a kid's level.

HOMEWORK HELP

http://school.discovery.com/ homeworkhelp/bjpinchbeck

This site boasts homework help by linking to well over six hundred web sites that provide help. The site claims "If you can't find it here, then you just can't find it."

MAGIC SCHOOL BUS

http://www.scholastic.com/magicschoolbus

Go to the Activity
Lab to play a num-
ber of games and
enjoy some activi-
ties. Or, learn more
about the Magic

School Bus and post some of your own art in
the Magic School Bus art gallery.

NOTES

_____

_____

_____

_____

_____

_____

DR. UNIVERSE

http://www.wsu.edu/druniverse

Why does electricity shock? How do mirrors work? Why are flowers colored the way they are? Find out answers  from the smartest cat you've ever seen.

NOTES

_____

_____

_____

_____

_____

_____

NOTES

_____

_____

_____

_____

_____

_____

_____

_____

_____

_____

_____

_____

_____

_____

JUST PLAIN
FUN SITES

MAMAMEDIA

http://www.mamamedia.com

Kids love what some call *the* place for kids on the Internet. Create cartoons, play challenging games, make wacky creatures, paint digital pictures, design and send animated cards. It's easy to spend hours at Mamamedia.

NOTES

_____

_____

_____

_____

_____

KIDCHATTERS

http://www.kidchatters.com

Here are clean, safe, and secure family-friendly chat rooms for kids. KidChatters' value is in keeping kids safe, happy, and productive on-line. You'll also find an article to read about chatting safely.

GAMES

http://www.zeeks.com

Zeeks.com is a free, all-in-one Internet destination for kids ages 6–13. Once here, they'll have fun, talk to other kids, do research, play games, and surf the Web. This site also offers its own Internet filtering software that you can subscribe to.

KIDZONKS

http://www.aol.kidzonks.com

Here you'll find the tremendous power of America Online packaged in a kid-sized site. Discover cool games and activities, great music, E-cards, funny comics and lots and lots more. You *don't* need to be an AOL member to use the site!

NOTES

_____

_____

_____

_____

_____

CRAYOLA

http://www.crayola.com/kids

You'll find everything you need to make your own cards—everything except the crayons, that is. If you provide the crayons, you'll enjoy an Activity Book with coloring sheets, card making info, and other creative ideas

YAHOO FOR KIDS

http://www.yahooligans.com

This is a terrific web guide for kids. With parental guidance, this search engine can help you find the sites you are looking for.

YAHOOLIGANS! GAMES

http://games.yahoo.com/games/

Play Go Fish, Chess, Backgammon, Tic-Tac-Toe, and many other games against other kids around the world.

NOTES

_____

_____

_____

_____

_____

_____

_____

_____

SQUIGLY'S PLAYHOUSE

http://www.squiglysplayhouse.com

Squigly's Playhouse
is a fun and safe
place for kids to play
and learn. You'll find
lots of things to do
here—including
laughing at jokes and riddles. You'll find games,
pencil puzzles, a writing corner, crafts, jokes,
coloring pictures, and brainteasers.

KIDS' VOICES

http://www.kidscom.com

Who said kids don't have a voice? This site
allows kids to write to a world leader, make new
friends from around the world, answer polls,
and take weekly writing challenges.

TV, MUSIC, MOVIES

http://www.cartoonnetwork.com

Do the Flintstones, Daffy Duck, or Tom and Jerry make you laugh? You'll find over two thousand cartoons, including storyboards, clips from TV shows and new web-based shows.

NOTES

_____

_____

_____

_____

_____

_____

NICKELODEON

http://www.nick.com

Kids can visit their favorite Nickelodeon characters on-line. In addition to specials, you can play games, look at pictures, listen to audio downloads, and download screensavers featuring all the Nickelodeon shows and movies. There's lots of opportunity to tell Nickelodeon what *you* think of their shows.

YOU CAN DO IT!

http://www.cyberkids.com

This site exists to help kids express themselves. This site encourages kids to submit art and drawings to be posted on-line. Kids are also encouraged to write and post their written work for everyone to see.

BEANIE BABIES

http://www.ty.com

It's hard to find a
kid who does not
have at least one
Beanie Baby. This
site offers more bean
bag info than you

can imagine—all from the makers of the
authentic Beanie Baby.

NOTES

_____

_____

_____

_____

_____

_____

KRISTY'S DESKTOP CREATIONS FOR KIDS

http://www.kwebdesign.com/kdesk

This page was designed to encourage young computer lovers to personalize their computers with original icons, cursors, and desktops. Includes downloadable examples and graphic resources.

KIDDONET

http://www.kiddonet.com

Through KiddoNet, children can explore the good aspects of the Internet without gaining access to inappropriate sites and material. Within this wholesome atmosphere, children navigate the Internet with a kid-friendly browser.

SEUSSVILLE

http://www.randomhouse.com/seussville

Spend time with
Sam-I-Am, Horton,
and the Whos. This
on-line funland
invites you to play
games with your

favorite Suessville friends, chat with the Cat in
the Hat, and win prizes.

NOTES

_____

_____

_____

_____

_____

_____

K.E.W.L.

http://www.cybercomm.net/~teach

This K.E.W.L. site stands for Kids' Excellent Web Links. This is a good starting point that links to kids sites on sports, literature, science, museums and other web-based activities.

NOTES

_____

_____

_____

_____

_____

_____

YOU RULE SCHOOL

http://www.youruleschool.com

Click on here to find the "Internet school where kids rule!" It's all fun and games—no homework—brought to you by General Mills, the company that makes Cheerios, Lucky Charms, Fruit Roll-Ups, and all kinds of other foods you probably eat all the time.

NOTES

_____

_____

_____

_____

_____

_____

_____

LINK MANIA

http://www.beritsbest.com

The same people who created Theodore Tugboat have created this site. If you start at this site you can plan on spending hours following the links to many topics that interest you: holidays, crafts, bugs, music, movies, and more.

FROG LAND

http://www.allaboutfrogs.org

Like frogs? Find some funny frog jokes and cartoons, or submit a picture of your own frog for nomination of "frog of the month." Learn all kinds of frog facts, take part in a silly frog poll, read some amazing stories about frogs, and learn how to better care for your own frog.

FOX KIDS

http://www.foxkids.com

Capture the best of FoxKids programming. Then join their club after you've played a few games and read their on-line magazine for kids.

NOTES

_____

_____

_____

_____

_____

_____

THE LEMONADE STAND

http://www.coolmath4kids.com/

This addicting game teaches you how to run a small business. Kids learn math and business skills—including just-in-time delivery and the laws of supply and demand.

THOMAS THE TANK ENGINE

http://www.thomasthetankengine.com

Thomas the Tank Engine is a young child's favorite. Here's the official site dedicated to the silly train and all the passenger cars, freight cars, and the scary diesels of his magical world.

WORLD VILLAGE KIDS

http://www.worldvillage.com/kidz

This home for kids of all ages features links specifically for boys and for girls. Kids can join the kids club and learn how to build their own home page. While on the site you can take a few moments and send a musical E-card to a friend.

NOTES

_____

_____

_____

_____

_____

EXPRESS YOURSELF!

http://www.bconnex.net/~kidworld

Enter the monthly writing contest, sing some karaoke, or just sit back and read stories written by other kids. Prefer cooking instead? Submit your favorite recipes or learn to cook from other young chefs. There's also a lesson on how to build your own home page—a lesson written by, you guessed it, another kid.

THEODORE THE TUGBOAT

http://www.cochran.com/theodore

Here's the home of the world's friendliest tugboat. There's lots to see and do with Theodore and his friends. Help Theodore and his friends make choices about how to spend the day at Big Harbour.

SPORTS INFO

http://members.aol.com/msdaizy/
sports/locker.html

Do you have a
favorite sport?
Whether you're a
football or baseball
fan, whether you
prefer basketball or

gymnastics, you'll find information on your
favorite sport. Use this site to get your sport's
history, official rules, referee signals, and some
skills and drills.

NOTES

_____

_____

_____

_____

PLAYGROUND GAMES

http://www.gameskidsplay.net

Here you can find rules for playground games (Red Rover, Mother May I?, Steal the Bacon, etc.) and verses for jump rope rhymes. You'll also find a link the American Kickball Association and their official rulebook.

ALL MIXED UP GAMES

http://www.allmixedup.com

Here are classic games you can play against the computer: hangman, Othello, tic-tac-toe, chess, and checkers. If you're in the mood for a game, this is a good place to be!

Paper Projects

http://www.ptialaska.net/~bundyd/paper.html

Looking to do something creative? This site will give you creative ideas of things you can create with paper. Start with coloring pages, move to origami, make a flying machine, and end with papier mâché.

Notes

_____

_____

_____

_____

_____

_____

_____

THE PUZZLE FACTORY

http://www.thepuzzlefactory.com

If you like mind-benders and brainteasers, here's your spot. You can solve mind-numbing problems and assemble jigsaw puzzles. If you like the site, you can send a puzzle E-card to a friend.

SWEET STUFF

http://www.hersheys.com/kidztown/

Chocolate-maker Hershey offers games, recipes, and the inside scoop on the favorite candies at this interactive site. You can even download candy-oriented screensavers!

COLLECTING FUN

http://kidscollecting.about.com/kids/
kidscollecting/

Collect baseball cards? Stamps? Rocks, bugs,
or kites? Kids' Collecting at About.com is the
place to learn all about collecting.

NOTES

_____

_____

_____

_____

_____

_____

_____

What a Great Kid

http://www.greatkids.com

Wherever you browse, you can find a great kid on this site. Log on to read about the cool contributions kids make in the world

Microsoft Kids

http://kids.msn.com

Microsoft has invented a web community for kids. Select your age level, and you are transported to appropriate activities, learning, and games—all done with Microsoft style.

COW PUZZLES

http://www.cartooncorner.com

Part of this site is hosted by Peetie Heffer, your own puzzle-loving host. Test your memory, search for clues, and refuse to be stumped by a cow.

NOTES

_____

_____

_____

_____

_____

_____

INVESTING FOR KIDS

http://library.thinkquest.org/3096

This site teaches the basics of stocks and bonds, introduces young investors to the stock market, as well as some other basics of investing. Future accountants can play the Think Quest Stock Game—a simulated stock trading game.

ALFY

http://www.alfy.com

 Come play at Alfy's playground and enjoy one of the most popular kids' sites on the net. Visit the arcade, the music box, and uncover all kinds of surprises that jump out at you.

GARFIELD

http://www.garfield.com

Here's your favorite cartoon cat! Log on to read the Garfield Gazette or check in with the Garfield fan club. While on-line, be sure to watch some Garfield TV and explore the Garfield E-mail service.

NOTES

Fun Island

http://www.funisland.com

Education and entertainment are smashed together in this engaging site. Games include word search, Tetris, and a bunch of board games you can play on-line (which means you won't have to find all the plastic pieces).

Weekly Reader

http://www.weeklyreader.com

Kids will enjoy visiting this site regularly because articles, polls, glossaries, and activities are updated to reflect national and world news.

AMERICAN GIRL

http://www.americangirl.com

If you know who Felicity, Addy, Kirsten, and Samantha are, you're probably in with these American Girls. Visit often for weekly updates and learn more about some of these friends and see what American Girl activities might be going on near you.

NOTES

_____

_____

_____

_____

_____

SUNDAY LAUGHS

http://www.comics.com

What's the best part of the Sunday paper? If you said the comics, then this is your site. Log on daily to catch up with Snoopy and the gang, B.C., and other favorites.

LEGO

http://www.lego.com

If you're a Lego nut, here's a great place to get ideas and fuel your creativity. If you're a novice with Lego, then you have plenty to learn from your adventures in Legoland. And if you think Legos are just for boys, then check out the part of this site made just for *girls*.

NOGGIN

http://www.noggin.com

Noggin TV at its best: Doug and The Wild Side. You can bust your noggin with riddles, wordamorphosis, and headbuzzers.

NOTES

_____

_____

_____

_____

_____

_____

Winner!

http://www.games.com

Here's a site to visit with your parents nearby. Check out and play games like Battleship, Sorry!, Monopoly, and Chinese Checkers. What makes these games extra fun? You'll play them against real live opponents scattered all over the world. You'll find text boxes where players can chat with each other while they play.

McDonalds

http://www.mcdonalds.com/mcdonaldland

McDonald's playland has grown beyond the ball pit and slide. Log on to see how big the playland has actually become. You won't get bored of the site quickly as there are lots of nooks, crannies, and hidden links to explore.

MORE THAN JUST COOKIES

http://www.nabiscokids.com

This graphically
intense site is a little
slow to load. But if
you're patient,
you can invent your
own screensaver and

explore the imagination station. Take a few
minutes to help make some cookies and use the
chip blaster to save your new cookies from an
out-of-control conveyor belt!

NOTES

_____

_____

_____

_____

_____

Holiday Info

http://www.kidsdomain.com/kids/html

What do Christmas, Thanksgiving, Presidents' Day, and Labor Day have in common? No school! Log on to research the background and history of the best days of the year!

Hot Wheels

http://www.hotwheels.com

 Ever collect virtual cars? Log on to see how to expand your virtual collection, join the birthday club, and download Hotwheels screensavers.

4KIDS

http://4kids.org

Think the Internet is cool? Like technology? Gadgets your thing? This site organizes Internet and technology news that's relevant to kids, reviews cool sites, and answers questions about your favorite web sites. There's even a spot to ask your own questions about all this stuff.

NOTES

_____

_____

_____

_____

_____

M&M'S

http://www.m-ms.com

What color M&M is your favorite? Catch up with your Red, Yellow, and Blue stars at the on-line home of your favorite candy.

AFRICAN AMERICAN HISTORY

http://www.afroam.org/children/children.html

 How much influence does African history have in our country? More than you think. Log on to learn more about African American heritage and its impact in our world.

NOTES

_____

_____

_____

_____

_____

_____

_____

_____

_____

_____

_____

_____

_____

_____

Notes

_____

_____

_____

_____

_____

_____

_____

_____

_____

_____

_____

_____

_____

_____